THE ORTHODOX

THE ORTHODOX
By Germi Flynn D. Garfin

THE ORTHODOX

> If you purchased this book without a cover you should be aware that the book is stolen property. It was reported as unsold and destroyed" to the publisher, and neither the author nor the publisher has received any payment for this "stripped book"

ISBN 978-1-105-80922-4

GERMI FLYNN D. GARFIN PUBLICATION 2012

Copyright © 2012 by GERMI FLYNN D. GARFIN.

All rights reserved. No part of this work covered by the copyright hereon may be reproduced or used in any form or by any means—graphic, electronic, or mechanical, including photocopying, recording, taping or information storage and retrieval systems—without the written permission of the publisher.

All characters in this book have no existence outside the imagination of the author and have no relation whatsoever to anyone bearing the same name or names. They are not even distantly inspired by any individual known or unknown to the author, and all incidents are pure invention.

This edition published and arranged with
GERMI FLYNN D. GARFIN

Printed in the USA.

THE ORTHODOX

TO MY INSPIRATIONS

THE ORTHODOX

CHAPTER ONE

Hi to everyone I wrote this book in order to inform you about what I discovered in my life. The content of this book will show you how I

THE ORTHODOX

handled very familiar obstacles in our life.

When I was born, of course my parents were so happy and if I could just see their faces I could probably explain it to you the caring that they had for me.

They wanted to see me as their masterpiece and maybe they were right because they were my parents.

THE ORTHODOX

They don't want me to start with a mistake in life. And that is why they started to correct me for everything even the one that God had given to me genetically. I was born left-handed and they noticed it right away when I was about at the age of four.

They don't want me to be left-handed when I grow up. I didn't notice the things they had done to me to keep me right-handed but they

THE ORTHODOX

told me when I was growing up that they use to tie my left hand in order not to use it by me especially when we were on meal time.

They repeatedly do it until such time that they had succeeded, I became adept as right-handed until now.

First of all, I did not write this book in order to be noticed by my parents on things that they have done to me. In fact I love them very much and

THE ORTHODOX

always thank them for the things that they have that reflects in me because they are the major influences that I discovered this secrets in life and if I will finish this book they will be the one that I assigned to edit and finalized my book.

I wrote this book in order that the people will know that a slightest force of change that we have done into our life will have a big impact

THE ORTHODOX

for us in the up and coming future and to be able to help them to solve this unseen mystery of outbreak even before in the age of time.

Even before in the ancient civilization there is already an outbreak of third sex such as gays and lesbians. In the bible, if I may recall Sodom and Gomorrah was the one proof that they already existed even before. I was able to come into

THE ORTHODOX

this idea because I want it to be stopped. Enough is enough.

In Sodom and Gomorrah it is very clear that they were punished by God because they were already a plague that knows no boundary at that time. Just in a matter of time they will spread in the whole world. And so God rained down fire to destroy Sodom and Gomorrah.

At present, it is already starting to wide spread in the whole world even

THE ORTHODOX

a thousand times as many as the Sodom and Gomorrah. Let me rephrase you with this. They may not be giving birth but they are still spreading. It means that they are sins or mistakes from the past that returns to us in a form of complex reactions. That might be because of a very slightest thing that God give to you and suddenly changes because you or your parents thinks it is not the way it should be. Well for me it is

THE ORTHODOX

not so bad at all, if you examine the writer carefully of this book.

It's obviously related to that kind of story a left-handed who became right-handed. That's how he discovered this right? "And everything else comes very easy for him!"

So how can we change the things that even time could not erase not even the story of Sodom and Gomorrah?

THE ORTHODOX

"Well I tell you this. If it will have to start it with me then I will do it. And the time is now."

First, let's start from identifying them, how it comes out and why? We all know that it could start even at the early age. At about ten years old. It is the common age of transformation to a person who started it so young.

THE ORTHODOX

For me, I could say that this boy inherited it to his father. His father might not be gay or somewhat he hides it in him and of course never told anyone about it but himself.

This is the side effect of not solving this outbreak. If it will not comes out on you it will be out on your siblings because it is like a curs that has to be cure. So how will you cure the one that was not even hurt you? Or can you call it sickness even you didn't feel any pain at all? Or you might

THE ORTHODOX

think that it is just normal to you to mesmerize with the same sex because of the fact that they are already accepted in our societies?

And that's the time you will know that you had a mistake in life or in the past maybe not with you but might be with the parental guidance either accidentally or intentionally.

It is often neglected because for me it doesn't really hurt and some people

THE ORTHODOX

just don't solve problems that were almost not a problem or negligible to him/her and just consider it as a part of his/her life. After all, what is life without small struggles?

In doing this you will not actually helping yourself but even worsens it due to the fact that you're ignoring it. Sooner or later your sons or daughters will be gays or lesbian respectively.

THE ORTHODOX

Another case of third sex happens on aged. Meaning it could happened to a person that has normally do not accept that they are gay but only to give up when they are already aging.

In this case I admire the patience of a person who suffered this faith because even though they have given up. They give it up with a fight. Or maybe they are bored on their life that's why they want to explore the beauty of the other world.

THE ORTHODOX

Example In some cases like this, a gay give it up for a friend that he wanted or he wanted to be with. And most of the time he was called gay for his wanted to be friend and in order to be friend with them. He eventually acknowledges himself as gay. This is a case that he never gives up without his intended intentions, to be part of the group.

THE ORTHODOX

I also observed in this case that something in his previous formula really works well so he didn't just give up in early fights. If we can even call it a fight as we know it. Some of them will turn sixty year old first before they called themselves as gays. And that is a fact that they had the right formula that they used in their life. But then again due to a boring life they switch to some thing they did not explored before.

THE ORTHODOX

If you ask me are they common to all even rich and poor? I say yes. This is common to all because even rich you could be subject to this outbreak. It is not about the money that you have. It is about how you understand it. Even if you are poor but you definitely understand the causes of it you will be save to it.

And take not on this. If you hide it and did not even try to cure it by understanding it. It will be

THE ORTHODOX

transferred to your offspring's. But if you understand this thing the way that I do you and your family will be saved by it. And you will notice the great changes that will be given to you by reading my book.

Okay, let's start on how gays and lesbian feels. Unfortunately the feeling of lesbians of course they feel that they are man. But There are some incident that a lesbian often

THE ORTHODOX

time give up their virginity to their so called friends.

They mingled with their friends drink with each other and she if the timing is right she will be gang banged. And end up being pregnant without even knowing who the father of her child is.

This is just some of the scenario that a woman did not really give up herself to be a man. But she wanted

THE ORTHODOX

to be a woman but for some reason she wants to be with the man's presence. In the end, she really wanted to be a mother. She is really true to herself.

For almost all gay, they seemed sure to their feelings that they were woman who were trap in the man's body.

In fact one of a friend of mine is a gay, we ask him to be a man and get married. He strictly says he doesn't

THE ORTHODOX

want to be man and don't want get married by women saying it as if he was almost vomited. He is a girl she said to us.

And seems there is no one who can change that fact on him. My co-worker said that to him because he really looks handsome and at first glance you can't even say to him that he is a gay.

THE ORTHODOX

In my applied solution to all of this, you will learn how it happens to a man or a woman without even noticing it. The answer will be very self explanatory and can be practiced right away when you read it. This is just short, but very much fruitful and if you apply it with your life. We will have a healthy lifestyle that's waiting for all of us! God Bless!!!

THE ORTHODOX

CHAPTER TWO

(The reasons why it happen to a man or a woman)

THE ORTHODOX

Brain *is* *intelligence*

Intelligence *comes from our* *curiosity* *as a human*

Curiosity *was captured by our observation implicating our own*

THE ORTHODOX

Judgment *base on gathered facts and experiences to a given object.*

Judgment *limits our decisions into one potential truth whether it is by evidence, experiences or what we had witnessed base on our* *Laws and Principles* *in life. Then we provide a* *conclusion* *based on every observation we'd make.*

THE ORTHODOX

Conclusions *are the one that influence the entire* **human race**.

Human race *through* **conclusions** *can be affected and can very dependent base on the gathered* **intelligence**.

Intelligence *has its direct influence to the gender preferences of a person, if it's not notice during its adolescence and events on its entire life.*

THE ORTHODOX

CHAPTER THREE

(THE MAJOR INFLUENCES)

THE ORTHODOX

MAJOR INFLUENCES:

Human senses are all connected to our brain prove it direct effect to us.

1. Sense of Sight
2. Sense of Hearing
3. Sense of Touch

Sense of Sight - as it changes your brain use unnoticed by you.

THE ORTHODOX

As far as I know, almost all male who became gay is left-handed. Let say they had an inclination to be left-handed.

But they change from orthodox stance. In that way, something in their consciousness developed to become what they are. For example, if you are a left-handed converted to an Orthodox stance.

THE ORTHODOX

Your genetic conditions or design on your body in which you are a left-handed will somehow show its superiority even though he is not in a major use as you prepared it. It is because you were designed to it and God give it to you as a unique human being.

If you ever heard about a "Brain Test" a spinning lady so to speak you will notice that your brain change in some series of tests. See Image.

THE ORTHODOX

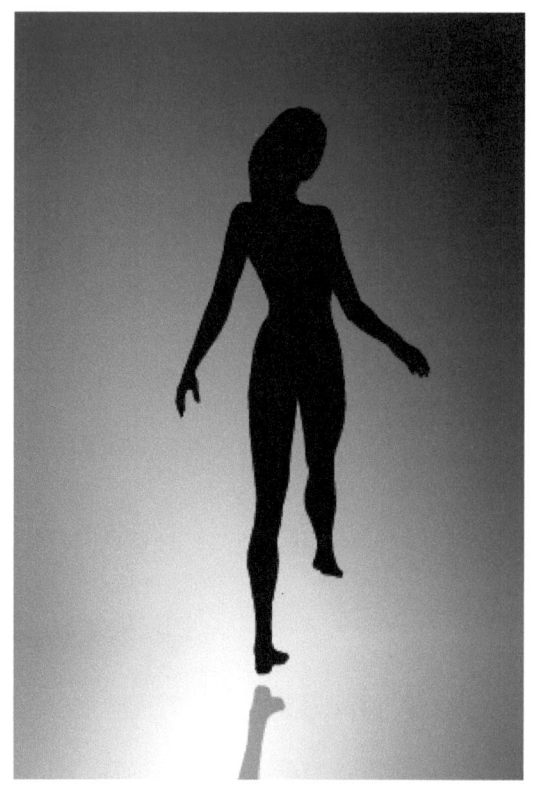

Spinning Lady

THE ORTHODOX

Sense of Hearing - as it changes your brain use unnoticed by you.

Hearing contributes a man to become Gay especially if they start at right at the age, as adolescence. This is because of Idolatry. Famous persons or great actors being praised with their big names.

At this point also, you where seeking for an attention on your crush on opposite sex and suddenly loose it to

THE ORTHODOX

a so called much better one for example you loose her to a man having name of Van Damme or Jericho.

 If this happen to a man very often as his attempt to court a girl then.

All of a sudden you are forever trap in that kind of environment and whenever you hear a famous name in your thought. It would shock you.

THE ORTHODOX

And now you are staggered by big names. This will help you to conclude when you don't know about the reason of it. If you ever watch a movie Peter Pan. You will now how and old man (Captain Hook) got puzzled in his thoughts. Through its hearing got invaded by a very big name in never land called Peter Pan. And of course this is all related in the above causes. See Image...

THE ORTHODOX

Captain Hook

Sense of Touch - as it changes your brain use unnoticed by you.

THE ORTHODOX

Touch if abused can be a great factor to become gay because when it is abused, it cannot identify the difference between a sensational touch and normal touch.

This might also occur in a rape victim trying to hide everything from it, they become insensitive to their feelings. One of the other things is the unnoticed cause of abusing our sense of touch.

THE ORTHODOX

It happened when a close relative is very much close to you having her skin or his (gay) skin get into your adolescent skin that tends yourself to react or to choose on what to do and a sensation to your skin develops through a skin of other person(cousin).

This what makes them very effective because in this situation. No one is prohibiting it in front of the family because it looks very normal to

THE ORTHODOX

cousins being closed to each other. So this will also rack the world of a man, when a skin tends to long it or find that sensation and becomes very addictive. And of course these are also in relation to above causes.

End

THE ORTHODOX